HOW TO TURN ADVERSITY INTO PROSPERITY

VICTORIA GRACE

Psalm 128:2 You will enjoy the fruit of your labor. How joyful and prosperous you will be!

THANKS AND ACKNOWLEDGEMENTS

Greetings to you all in the Name of our Lord and Saviour, Jesus Christ; I pray your life is filled with joy and happiness......

I would like to take this time to thank and acknowledge the following important people in my life. My husband Joe for his constant encouragement, and my daughters Davina and Danica as they serve as my inspirations. These two young ladies inspired me to keep my faith in the Lord Jesus Christ. As I looked at their innocent faces and watched them put their faith in Jesus Christ at the very young age has inspired me to grow and strengthen my faith in God. I also thank my parents. Finding joy in every circumstance.

This book came about in my daily devotion and reading of the bible everyday. God is righteousness, peace, and joy in the Holy Ghost. Hope is the life-spring of joy and full of hope. When I look at my life...I am where I am, where Christ wants me to be. Amid turmoil and trouble...Christ is with me; I have inner peace...I have inner joy. In sadness and disappointment, through it all, Jesus Christ is guiding me, caring for me, and loving me. Christ is indeed all around me. Rejoice in the Lord always.

ABOUT THE AUTHOR

Victoria Grace is a dedicated and faithful servant of the Lord Jesus Christ, Sunday school teacher (children and adults), Homegroup Leader, Life Coach, Christian Motivational Speaker, author, educator, and Ladies Group Facilitator. My experience in social services for twenty years has given me different perspectives in life and the world. In my free time, I like spending my time outdoors as I enjoy nature and photography, which is my hobby. My writing derives from my everyday life experiences and is inspired by reading the words of God (Bible) everyday.

Through Jesus Christ, who gives me strength, I can face the reality of my past, lay everything down at the feet of Jesus. To forgive myself as the Lord has forgiven me. Through all my life experiences. God is always there with me, loving me as it says in Jeremiah 29:11 "For I know the plans I have for you," declares the Lord, "plans to prosper you and not to harm you, plans to give you hope and a future.

TABLE OF CONTENTS

THANKS, AND ACKNOWLEDGEMENTS 3
ABOUT THE AUTHOR 4
PREFACE 6
CHAPTER 1 POVERTY AFFECTS GENERATIONS 8
CHAPTER 2 SEE YOUR LIFE THROUGH HEAVEN'S EYES. 14
CHAPTER 3 PROCRASTINATION 19
CHAPTER 4 WHAT IS THE PURPOSE OF LIFE? 25
CHAPTER 5 ARE YOU ENJOYING LIFE TO THE FULLEST? 32
CHAPTER 6 TRUST AND CONTENTMENT 38
CHAPTER 7 ARE YOU GRATEFUL FOR EVERYTHING? 45
CHAPTER 8 TAKE NOTHING FOR GRANTED 53
CONCLUSION: 61

PREFACE

THE BOOK OF ECCLESIASTES IS A GREAT BOOK TO FIND WISDOM ON THE JOURNEY TO PROSPERITY. A BOOK WHERE YOU CAN FIND KNOWLEDGE TO RISE FROM POVERTY TO PROSPERITY.

In this profound book, Solomon takes us on a mental journey through his life, and he explained that everything he tried, tested, or tasted was useless, irrational, pointless, foolish, and empty, an exercise in futility. Remember, these words are from one who had it all...power, wisdom, and wealth.

When Solomon became king, he asked God for wisdom (2 Chronicles 1:7-12), and he became the wisest man in the world (1 King 4:29-34). He studied, taught, judged, and wrote. Kings and leaders from other nations came to Jerusalem to learn from him. But, with all his practical insight on life, Solomon failed to heed his own advice, and his life began its downward spiral.

Near the end of his life, he looked back with an attitude of humility and repentance. Solomon hopes to spare his readers the bitterness of learning through personal experience that everything apart from God is empty, hollow, and meaningless.

The tone of Ecclesiastes is negative and pessimistic. The entire book is filled with practical wisdom (how to accomplish things in life and stay out of trouble) and spiritual wisdom (how to find and know eternal values). The futility of life is there for a purpose---to lead people to seek true happiness in God alone. All these temporal things in life must be seen in the light of eternity.

Life is not found in knowledge, money, pleasure, work, or popularity. Ecclesiastes shows the path in life that leads to emptiness and helps us discover true purpose in life. True contentment comes from knowing God and His purpose for our lives.

Fear God throughout your life and fill your life with serving God and others. The cure for emptiness is to centre on God. Dedicate your life in serving the Lord Jesus Christ.

CHAPTER 1
POVERTY AFFECTS GENERATIONS

Ecclesiastes 9:11

I returned and saw under the sun that the race is not to the swift, nor the battle to the strong, neither yet bread to the wise, nor yet riches to men of understanding, nor yet favour to men of skill; but time and chance happened to them all.

Mankind has twisted life. We make it to what God did not intend, and then we say life is unfair. It isn't difficult to see that the swiftest or the fastest always win, the wise remain poor, and the skillful are unknown for their talents. Let us then reduce our expectations in this imperfect world. Remind ourselves that we live in a fallen world.

Poverty passes on from generation to generation. Some do see this a big problem in our society; some would just simply ignore this problem. Many homes and families are torn apart due to impoverish life. We can not call poverty a lifestyle as it is something. We can irradicate if human race works together and treats one another as equal. Everyone should be accountable for one another. Do we blame our poor existence to our ancestors, governments, or to our general system, or shall we blame ourselves for not working hard enough to get out of poverty.

We often misinterpret poverty to being needy. Yes, our government should implement some sort of prevention resources and educate humans. Educating people is imperative and a must for a person to be a productive member of the society. On the other hand, the system that suppose to protect its people is the ones that exclude such less fortunate people. Shall we then make our government accountable for our misfortune? Are we asking too much, but we are doing very little for ourselves?

Many families are torn apart by the system, whether by choice or by force. If the government utilizes prevention through intervention and education. Perhaps few families will be living in an impoverish environment. Ironically, as some people look at the less fortunate as an outcast in the society. However, poverty is not limited to money or material things that money can buy. One can also be impoverished with love and/or spiritual.

Ecclesiastes 2:11

Yet when I surveyed all that my hands had done and what I had toiled to achieve, everything was meaningless, a chasing after the wind; nothing was gained under the sun.

In all our attempt finding life's meaning, in all our accomplishments, as if we are chasing the wind. We feel the wind as it passes, but we can't catch hold of it or keep it. Our good feelings are only temporary. Think about what we consider worthwhile in our lives (time, money, and energy). Will we one day look back and say that these were chasing the wind? Security and self-worth are not found in these earthly accomplishments but far beyond them in the love of God. Seeking wisdom has definite advantages in this life. But the most important knowledge is found in knowing the infinite God.

Growing up in poverty. Thus, I know how it feels to be an outcast and have nothing. When I was growing up, some people looked down on me and my family. Some even look at me as if insignificant, no-good person who will amount to nothing and will not accomplish anything in this world. Each day was struggle, and everyday also was another chance to trust in the Lord. I know what it is to be in need, and I know what it is to have plenty. I have learned the secret of being content in any and every situation, whether well fed or hungry, whether living in plenty or in want. (Philippians 4:12-20).

Ecclesiastes 1:18

The greater my wisdom, the greater my grief. To increase knowledge only increases sorrow.

Sometimes, we feel that our eyes are fountain of tears. We are filled with emotions of disappointment and discouragement. We weep in despair, and our hearts bleed with sorrow. Gone are the melodies of birds singing. And our future seems bleak. God sees our troubles and hears our cries. We can rest in God's arms. In Christ alone, we have hope, and our future is bright.

The behaviour and custom of this world are usually selfish and often corrupt. Our refusal to conform to the world must be deeper than our behaviour and custom. It must be firmly bound in our minds. We are to be transformed by the renewal of our minds. It is possible to rise from poverty and be prospered and enjoy the blessing of the Lord.

God has a good, pleasing, and perfect plan for his people. He wants us to be new people with a freshness of thought, alive to glorify him. Since God wants only what is best for us. He gave us his only Son, Jesus Christ to make our new life possible. We should joyfully accept the newness of our being. Only when our minds are renewed by the new attitude Christ gives us are we truly transformed. We can break the chain of poverty.

Approach your decisions from an eternal perspective - consider the impact now and forever. Live a life with an attitude that although this life is short, poverty reigns now; we can live with God forever through our Lord and Saviour, Jesus Christ. Rejoice every day, but remember that eternity is forever. A wise person does not think of the moment alone. It is a wonderful thing to be alive.

Ecclesiastes 5:10

He that loveth silver shall not be satisfied with silver; nor he that loveth abundance with increase: this is also vanity.

No one knew more than King Solomon, one of the richest men to ever live, how impossible it is for silver, gold, and all the things money can buy to satisfy one's soul. It is the very things that many cannot buy and that only God can give that are the most precious, most satisfying gifts of all. God is the giver of true riches that money could never buy. Only God can give peace, joy, love, faith, and all the fruits of the Spirit. When you give up worldly possessions and comforts for the sake of advancing the Kingdom of God, you will be rewarded, either in this life or in the next. May you see the true value and eternal riches more highly than the passing and deceitful riches of the earth. God gave us riches and freedom from poverty and enslavement through Jesus Christ and break the chain of poverty.

The fear of being labelled or judged as "poor" has left our culture with a lack of good judgement. The bible clearly tells us to judge rightfully. In our society, we appoint judges to judge those who break the law and are punished accordingly. It's often easier to magnify others' faults while ignoring our own. Jesus Christ tells us to examine ourselves and our lives first instead of criticizing others. Often, the traits that bother us in others are often the habits that we dislike in ourselves. If we are ready to criticize someone, check and see if we deserve the same criticism. Everyone is guilty of being "judgemental." Recognize that in this world, both good and evil people will experience judgement. But we can be assured that God will rightly judge and reward those who obey His commandments. The prideful and rebellious will also get their just rewards. One day, we will be judged, and we will be rewarded by God...if not now, in the life to come. God loves us, and he is just. Our complete judgement or reward may not be in this life---but it will happen.

Ecclesiastes 8:17

"I realized that no one can discover everything God is doing under the sun. Not even the wisest people discover everything, no matter what they claim."

Are we letting what we don't know about the future destroy the joy God gives today and miss out on the blessings of today? Even if we have access to the world's wisdom, the wisest man would know very little. There are always more questions than answers to life. However, the unknown should not cast shadows over our joy, faith, or work because God is in control, and we can put our trust in Him.

After accepting Christ as my Lord and Savior... yes, I am redeemed I am guaranteed eternal life. However, my Spiritual journey has just begun. The reign of the Holy Spirit is a must for my heart and mind to be transformed. It is a lifetime process as humans will not be rid of sins; I am forgiven---and yet I still also have the tendency to commit sins intentionally or unintentionally.

Being redeemed doesn't mean that God's works in us are complete. Therefore, abiding and reading the words of God daily is a must so that we are in constant communication with God, and the Holy Spirit will guide us to the path of righteousness. It is often misunderstood about redemption and being sinless. As we live life according to God's will and not ours, God will perfect us to attain his ultimate purpose in our lives to live a godly life. In this verse (Philippians 1:6 Being confident of this very thing, that he which hath begun a good work in you will perform it until the day of Jesus Christ:) meaning God will continue to guide us to live a life that is holy and acceptable to him until the end of the day.

As we continue to walk on this earth, we will continue to commit sins, but we have the assurance, as the bible stated in (1 John 1:9 If we confess our sins, he is faithful and just to forgive us our sins, and to cleanse us from all unrighteousness.) Therefore, we need not worry about our future in heaven because we are always forgiven of our sins. Keep abiding in Christ, and your path will always lead to righteousness. (Proverbs 3:5-6 Trust in the Lord with all your heart, and do not lean on your understanding. In all your ways, acknowledge him, and he will make straight your paths). You will be blessed.

What an amazing promise and unfathomable love God bestowed upon us. May God's blessings be yours always!!!!

Romans 15:13 Now may the God of hope fill you with all joy and peace in believing, so that you will abound in hope by the power of the Holy Spirit.

CHAPTER 2
SEE YOUR LIFE THROUGH HEAVEN'S EYES

Ecclesiastes 7:14

On a good day, enjoy yourself; On a bad day, examine your conscience. God arranges for both kinds of days. So that we won't take anything for granted.

God allows both adversity and prosperity to come into our lives. He blends them into our lives in such a way that we can't predict the future or count on human power and wisdom. In prosperity times, we love to give ourselves the credit. In adversity, we tend to blame God. When life appears certain, don't let pride make you too comfortable. God allows trials and tribulations to drive us back to him. When life seems uncertain, do not despair--God is in control and will bring good results out of tough times. We human; we have limited knowledge; therefore, we look for others to help us gain certain knowledge, and we hope that they will impart some sort of wisdom. Ecclesiastes 10:2 A wise man's heart directs him toward the right, but the foolish man's heart directs him toward the left. Proverbs 3:6 In all your ways acknowledge Him, And He shall direct your paths. To know our Heavenly Father as King David did is the most beautiful experience.

Ecclesiastes 5:19-20

19 Every man also to whom God hath given riches and wealth, and hath given him the power to eat thereof, and to take his portion, and to rejoice in his labour; this is the gift of God. 20 For he shall not much remember the days of his life; because God answereth him in the joy of his heart.

God wants us to view what we have (be it much or little) with the right perspective - our possessions are a gift from God. They are the reason to rejoice but not the source of our joy since every good thing comes from God. We should focus more on the giver than the gift. We can be content with what we have when we realize that with God, we have everything we need; all we must do is believe.

(Philippians 4:12 "I know what it is to be in need, and I know what it is to have plenty. I have learned the secret of being content in any and every situation, whether well fed or hungry, whether living in plenty or in want.") To be content is to see life from God's point of view. Focus on our priorities and be grateful for everything God has given us. Often, our desire to have more and the longing to fill the empty place in our life to have more lead us to discontent.

Ecclesiastes 11:7-8

Light is sweet, and it pleases the eyes to see the sun. 8 However many years a man may live, let him enjoy them all. But let him remember the days of darkness, for they will be many. Everything to come is meaningless.

It is a wonderful thing to be alive. Rejoice everyday, but remember that eternity is forever. A wise person does not think of the moment alone. Approach your decisions from an eternal perspective - consider the impact now and forever. Live a life with an attitude that although this life is short, we can live with God forever.

We often struggle because of our carelessness. We were once plagued by the broken image of our dreams and expectations. We struggle with self-esteem; thus, we must pray for the Lord to continue to conform us into the perfect image of our Jesus Christ. This takes our focus from ourselves and puts it on the Lord. We were made for God, not the world. (Genesis 1:26 Then God said, "Let us make mankind in our image, in our likeness, so that they may rule over the fish in the sea and the birds in the sky, over the livestock and all the wild animals, and overall, the creatures that move along the ground.")

Ecclesiastes 8:1

How wonderful it to be wise, to analyze and interpret things. Wisdom lights up a person's face, softening its harshness.

Wisdom is the ability to see life from God's perspective and to know the best course of action to take. Most of us would agree that wisdom is an asset, but how can we acquire it? We begin to learn and find wisdom through reverence and fear of God. Therefore, wisdom is a result of trusting and knowing God; not the way to find God. Knowing God will lead to understanding and sharing this knowledge with others.

You're so loved and beautiful beyond imagination! (2 Corinthians 3:18 And we, who with unveiled faces all reflect the glory of the Lord, are being transformed into His image with intensifying glory, which comes from the Lord, who is the Spirit.) No one can comprehend. Even you will never comprehend the great love that God has for you! You are not in the world for nothing. Your life is not meaningless. God created you for Himself. He wants you to experience His love, He wants to spend time with you, He wants to tell you the special things of His heart. God never intended for you to look for confidence in yourself.

Ecclesiastes 3:12-13

12 I know that nothing is better for them than to rejoice and to do good in their lives, 13 and also that every man should eat and drink and enjoy the good of all his labour—it is the gift of God.

Don't take life as a big irresponsible party...instead, take pleasure in what we are doing through God, and enjoy life as it is a gift from God. True enjoyment in life comes only as we follow

God's guidelines for living. We will truly enjoy life when one takes life each day as a gift from God, thanking God for it and serving him in it through our Lord Jesus Christ. (Ecclesiastes 5:12 The sleep of a labouring man is sweet, whether he eat little or much: but the abundance of the rich will not suffer him to sleep.) Do you ever think that if you become rich, all your problems would go away? We learn that wealth brings its own set of anxieties. Fear of theft and loss can rob a rich person of sleep and peace. But the one who is sustained with daily bread from the Lord rests in comfort, knowing that God meets all his needs.

Ecclesiastes 3:12

I know that there is nothing better for men than to be happy and do good while they live.

The ability to enjoy life is one of God's most excellent gifts, although we often abuse it. God wants us to enjoy life. When we have the proper view of God, we discover that real pleasure is not found in what we accumulate but enjoying whatever we have as gifts from God. The world has us comparing ourselves to each other. You don't need to prove to anyone how valuable you are. (1 Corinthians 6:20 You were bought at a price. Therefore, honour God with your bodies.) You were bought with the precious blood of our Lord Jesus Christ. Not only has God chosen you, not only has God saved you, but God is working in your struggles to make you more like Christ. Don't let things like sins, poverty, and insecurity discourage you. Now press on. Keep on fighting! Don't give up. (Galatians 6:9: "Let us not become weary in doing good, for at the proper time we will reap a harvest if we do not give up.")

Ecclesiastes 4:4

Then, I observed that most people are motivated to succeed because they envy their neighbours. But this, too, is meaningless– like chasing the wind.

Rather than looking to the world to patch up spiritual wounds, which it can never do, we should look to God to change our hearts. Nothing in this world will satisfy. Find satisfaction and joy in Christ, which remains forever. You can't try to substitute the joy found in Christ. All other joy is only temporary. God says, "I'm going to be your confidence" (Hebrews 10:35-36: "So do not throw away your confidence; it will be richly rewarded. You need to persevere so that when you have done the will of God, you will receive what he has promised.") It is important on our walk of faith that we get alone with God so we can allow God to work in us and through us in Christ Jesus. He never intended for you to look for confidence in yourself. Jesus Christ is the answer to all self-worth issues that may arise in your life. You are more to God than you can ever imagine! The gospel reveals your value. You are to die for! Jesus Christ bore our sins on the cross, and He died for you. (Jeremiah 29:11: "For I know the plans I have for you, declares the Lord, plans to prosper you and not to harm you, plans to give you hope and a future.")

2 Chronicles 15:7: "But as for you, be strong and do not give up, for your work will be rewarded."

CHAPTER 3
PROCRASTINATION

Ecclesiastes 11:4

Whoever watches the wind will not plant; whoever looks at the clouds will not reap.

What does the Bible say about Procrastination? There are many examples in Scripture of people avoiding their responsibilities and therefore, suffering the consequences. Whatever your hand finds to do, do it with all your might, for in the realm of the dead, where you are one day be going, there is neither working nor planning nor knowledge nor wisdom. The Word of God encourages us to labour honestly and diligently for the benefit of ourselves and others. May this Bible verse about procrastination inspire you to the action! (Proverbs 6:6-8 Go to the ant, you sluggard; consider its ways and be wise! It has no commander, no overseer or ruler, yet it stores its provisions in summer and gathers its food at harvest.)

Ecclesiastes 8:16-17

16 In my search for wisdom and in my observation of people's burdens here on earth, I discovered that there is ceaseless activity, day and night. 17 I realized that no one can discover everything God is doing under the sun. Not even the wisest people discover everything, no matter what they claim.

Even if we have access to the world's wisdom; the wisest man would know very little. There are always more questions than answers to life. However, the unknown should not cast shadows over our joy, faith, or work because God is in control, and we can put our trust in Him.

Are you enjoying life to the fullest? Are you grateful for everything? Do you take no one and nothing for granted? One theme in the poetic literature of the Bible is that God is incomprehensible; we can not know Him completely. But we can have knowledge about Him. The bible is full of details about who God is; how we can know Him, and we can have an eternal relationship with Him. We can never know enough to answer all of life's questions (Ecclesiastes 3:11 He has made everything beautiful in its time. He has also set eternity in the human heart; yet no one can fathom what God has done from beginning to end.), to predict our own future, or to manipulate God for our own ends. Life always has more questions than answers, and we must constantly go to God for fresh insights into life's dilemmas through Christ Jesus.

Ecclesiastes 12:13-14

13 *Let us hear the conclusion of the whole matter: Fear God and keep His commandments, For this is man's all.* **14** *For God will bring every work into judgment, Including every secret thing, Whether good or evil.*

Don't get impressed by earthly wealth, materials and possessions. For one day everything we hold dear and put value on can disappear in a blink of an eye. Thus, be thankful and content with the Lord's blessing each day.

Don't waste God's gifts. Without dependence on God and his guidance, even great ability is wasted. Even at a moment of great success, our pride, procrastination, and personal weaknesses are our greatest challenges. God has a purpose for every life, which becomes a real adventure for those who are willing to obey him wholeheartedly. When our attention is focused on God rather than our problems, God can help in unexpected ways. God's plan weaves live together in a pattern beyond our understanding. God uses our mistakes to fit into his plans. God is always in control of all that we desire. May it be for good that in the end, we may find ourselves glorifying God. For we are created to glorify God. Let us then love one another as God is love. Let love be our guide in all that we do and speak.

Ecclesiastes 7:9

Be not hasty in thy spirit to be angry: for anger resteth in the bosom of fools.

Are we reacting to an evil situation or action that you are going to set right? Are we responding selfishly to a personal insult? Anger can be like a fire out of control. It can burn us and consume everything in its path. Anger pushes us into hasty decisions that cause division, bitterness, and guilt. Anger is a legitimate reaction to injustice. When we feel that we treated unfairly, we feel angry. Pray that God will help us control our anger, channelling legitimate anger into effective action and conquering selfish anger through humility and repentance and avoid procrastination.

A miserable life - filled with trouble, pain, and misery - is a choice. Negative and discontented people choose to let circumstances and foolish feelings destroy their lives. Positive and contented people have a party most every day! We may face excruciating poverty, abundant wealth, and everything in between. Whatever the circumstance, we need to learn to be content; finding real joy should be the focus of all our attention and energy, knowing Jesus Christ and obeying Him. Our desire to know Christ above all else is wonderfully expressed in the following words: Philippians 3:8 "Everything else is worthless when compared with the priceless gain of knowing Jesus Christ my Lord. I have put aside all else, counting it worth less than nothing."

Ecclesiastes 8:9

All this I have seen and applied my heart to every work that is done under the sun: There is a time in which one man rules over another to his own hurt.

Having a right attitude about God can help us deal with present injustices in this world. Prosperity is not always good, and adversity is not always bad. But God is always good, if we live as God wants us to, we will experience contentment.

Our world is filled with injustice, poverty, war, and rebellion against God, all of which should move us to tears and spring us into actions -- to create peace among nations and among ourselves can cause us to procrastinate. As we see and hear what is happening around the world, God's protection is on His children. God is our refuge, a shelter when we are afraid. Our faith in God our Lord Jesus Christ, as PROTECTOR would carry us through all the dangers and fears of life. This should be a picture of our trust---trading all our fears for faith in our Lord Jesus Christ, no matter what kind of fear it may be. Realizing that life is short helps us use the little time we have more wisely. It helps us concentrate on using our lives for eternal good, not just for the pleasure of the moment. It may look like we are surrounded by enemies (evil), but the Lord surrounds us with love and protection. (John 16:33 These things I have spoken to you, that in Me you may have peace. In the world you will have tribulation; but be of good cheer, I have overcome the world.") All these God's promises should stop us from procrastinating.

Ecclesiastes 3:1

There is an appointed time for everything. And there is a time for every event under heaven--

After years of pleasing others. Perhaps it is time to take the covers from our dreams for change and, set our feet on another climb, and move forward. Fix our eyes on a different goal. Time for a change. Time to take a journey. Time to deal our self with the pleasure of things we like to do, to serve the Lord. Time to move forward...A simple statement, but hard to do. Time is now; moving forward is possible with courage, determination, and dedication. With God's help, we can move mountains. And change the course of our life's direction with the Lord's guidance.

Security and self-worth are not found in these earthly accomplishments but far beyond them in the love of God. Seeking wisdom has definite advantages in this life. But the most important knowledge is found in knowing the infinite God, our Lord Jesus Christ. (Job 36:26 - 30 Behold, God is great, and we know him not, neither can the number of his years be searched out. For he maketh small the drops of water: they pour down rain according to the vapour thereof: Which the clouds do drop and distil upon man abundantly. Also, can anyone understand the spreading of the clouds or the noise of his tabernacle? Behold, he spreadeth his light upon it, and covereth the bottom of the sea.)

Ecclesiastes 7:20

There is not a righteous person on earth who always does good and never sins.

We are not perfect. We have more faults than any good in us. Each day, we just trust God that He will walk with us to give us eyes to see goodness and beauty in all that we see. Each day, we pray that God gives us a heart full of love to all so we can love despite and regardless of what it may be. Each day, we should pray that our life is a beacon to all and that our characters will be worthy to emulate by others. Each day, we pray that the footsteps we leave behind will lead others to believe and be in God's love and light. Each day, we give ourselves to God and just trust Him with everything. Each day, we are thankful for everything. Each day, we pray because we know we are no better than others. We will stumble and fall. It's true we will sin and make mistakes, but we must never use this excuse to rebel against God's Word. Don't let the mistakes to deter us from moving forward and do what God wants us to do. Keep moving forward, and do not procrastinate.

Proverbs 22:13 The lazy person claims, "There's a lion out there! If I go outside, I might be killed!"

CHAPTER 4
WHAT IS THE PURPOSE OF LIFE?

Ecclesiastes 3:14 (KJV)

I know that whatsoever God doeth, it shall be forever: nothing can be put to it, nor anything taken from it: and God doeth it, that men should fear before him.

Our purpose of life starts with whom we know (knowing and glorifying God our Lord Jesus Christ), not what we know or how good we are. We should fear God. Fear does not mean we cringe in terror, but to respect, revere, and stand in awe of God... It is impossible to fulfill God-given purpose unless we fear God and give him first place in our lives. We are given a purpose to share God's love. Our lack of faith causes us to fear that the tasks given to us are unattainable. When we trust that nothing is impossible in God, then we can do our job easier. God loves each one of us even when we fail. Love God and love others.

Life's demand does get away with us, and we often neglect what really is important after God. We often tend to put aside those we claim to love and care. All in all, God is always glorified. Nothing brings greater joy than to serve the Lord. It is always my prayer that you will walk in the ways of the Lord and that your life will be a testimony for others that would lead them to believe and follow Christ as their Saviour and Lord. May the footsteps that you leave behind will lead others to believe in our Lord Jesus Christ.

Ecclesiastes 2:11

Yet when I surveyed all that my hands had done and what I had toiled to achieve, everything was meaningless, a chasing after the wind; nothing was gained under the sun.

The secret of a good attitude is filling our minds with good thoughts (pure, holy, and lovely). Thoughts dwell on the good things in life. As we face struggle each day, look at our attitude and examine what we allow to enter our mind and what we choose to dwell on. Our attitude colors our whole personality. We cannot always choose what happens to us, but we can choose our attitude towards each situation through Christ, our Savior and Lord.

In all our attempt finding life's meaning, in all our accomplishments as if we are chasing the wind. We feel the wind as it passes, but we can't catch hold of it or keep it. Our good feelings are only temporary. Think about what we consider worthwhile in our lives (time, money, and energy). Will we be one day look back and say that these were chasing the wind? Security and self-worth are not found in these earthly accomplishments but far beyond them in the love of God. Seeking wisdom has definite advantages in this life. But the most important knowledge is found in knowing the infinite God. Trust the Lord for everything and in every area of your life. As life always takes us in different directions, and God places us to wherever He thinks is best for us…

Ecclesiastes 12:14

For God will bring every work into judgment, Including every secret thing, Whether good or evil.

Are you enjoying life to the fullest? Are you grateful for everything? Do you take no one and nothing for granted? The ultimate source of all encouragement is the fact that God is love, and He loves us and has a perfect plan for us. How comforting to know and have the assurance of God's unfailing love for us. When God takes priority in our lives; life becomes an adventure. Even our mundane routine takes on meaning and promise because they hold a greater purpose. If you're bored in life, check your relationship with GOD.

Demonstrate an intimate familiarity with God's Word… ("Man shall not live on bread alone, but on every word that comes from the mouth of God." Matthew 4:4). When your thoughts and words are based on the Bible and not your opinion, balancing faith and actions on the word of God; rather learn to trust in the Savior Jesus Christ. When we let God's words guide us, we will get through life's struggles. Our burden will be light, and he restores our spirit. Have faith in God; He controls everything that goes in our lives through Christ Jesus.

Godliness, Common sense, or intelligence. What is more important??? ("Rather, it should be that of your inner self, the unfading beauty of a gentle and quiet spirit, which is of great worth in God's sight." 1 Peter 3:4). Don't frantically wring our hands in the valleys of the unexpected. We have the inner peace of the Holy Spirit to comfort, guide, and teach us when everything seems out of control. We learn to lay your concerns at the foot of the cross and leave them there. ("Be strong and courageous. Do not be afraid; do not be discouraged, for the Lord your God will be with you wherever you go." Joshua 1:9). As our culture tumbles down the slippery slope of worldliness and immorality, we are confident in our Sovereign God to make all things work together for good. Refuse to let fear invade our thoughts or feelings by constantly reminding ourselves of God's promise to never leave us. Be relentless in prayer and intercession… ("Pray continually." 1 Thessalonians 5:17).

Be generous in our resources… ("You will be enriched in every way so that you can be generous on every occasion…" 2 Corinthians 9:11). We will give time, energy, gifts, and finances in days of feasting or famine. We need to learn to resist the fear of holding back because of our strong confidence in God to meet our needs according to His riches in glory and to grant all our desires according to His will. Be driven to complete tasks thoroughly... ("Whatever your hand finds to do, do it with all your might." Ecclesiastes 9:10). Be fully committed to finishing everything we started to the best of our ability. Whether for home, job, or church—your dependability reflects the inner conviction of working for Jesus Christ and not for those around you. Your reputation becomes solid among believers as well as unbelievers. Each passing day holds a memory untold. Your life is a story that is yet to be completed as the final chapter is written by our creator. Don't let life pass you by taking it for granted.

Godliness, common sense, and intelligence are all equally important as we live life in this world where sins are prevalent and we are in a constant battle between good and evil. Let the Lord Jesus Christ guide you with His words using common sense and intelligence in a godly manner.

Ecclesiastes 7:16

Be not overly righteous, and do not make yourself too wise. Why should you destroy yourself?

Life can change in a blink of an eye. What we thought was important no longer matter as life changed unexpectedly. We often take things and people who love us for granted. As we sorrowfully sit with tears streaming down our cheeks, reminiscing the past. Our present predicament was because of our own carelessness and unwise decisions. God is always there to help and guide us. We often doubt God's power to deliver us; hence, we try to do everything on our own.

We regretfully think what we could have done differently. As a result, we live to regret our decisions. However, we can rely on God to help us make it better. We cannot change the past, but we can do our best in the present and hope for a better future. As sorrow and regret engulf us to the abyss of nothingness, remember God will never leave us nor forsake us. We have everything we need all we must do is believe, as we entwined our spirit with the Holy Spirit. The unfathomable love of God gives us second chance to make it better. Trust God through Christ Jesus he is in control of our destiny. (Proverbs 10:30 The righteous will never be shaken, but the wicked will not inhabit the land.)

Ecclesiastes 1:4

Generations come and generations go, but the earth remains forever.

Understand that for any given problem, there is a solution. Creative people come up with creative solutions. People who are willing, or need, to push out of their comfort zone. Prepare for a big change, re-educate ourselves (read our bible), and our way of thinking is almost a "lifestyle" change. Our willingness to take a new perspective toward day-to-day life's situations. Our ability to think differently with an open mind, thinking about the substance of issues, and being receptive to doing things differently. Through obedience in God's words. Focused on the value of finding new ideas and acting on it. Ready to strive to create values in newer ways. Our ability to listen, support, and nurture others. Being flexible and see through the gray area.

Negative attitudes and fear of failure are the biggest hurdles. Reflect on positive things instead and look at things differently (through God's eyes). Break free from the dull routine of day-to-day life. Find ways of minimizing routine in our life while we still embracing rituals. Expecting thing to never change, we are setting ourselves to a lot of pain and unhappiness when things and people do change around us without taking us along. We all heard it: "think outside of the box." However, we often deny that we are inside a box. We are stuck in a rut, and no matter how hard we try, we fall back into the rut. We can't come up with a solution to a nagging problem. (Psalm 125:1 They that trust in the LORD shall be as mount Zion, which cannot be removed, but abideth for ever.)

Ecclesiastes 9:1 (KJV)

For all this, I considered in my heart even to declare all this, that the righteous, and the wise, and their works, are in the hand of God: no man knoweth either love or hatred by all that is before them.

Many a time, I made plans for myself, my life, and my future. Some of my dreams came true; some are yet to come true; some may never materialize as God responds is NO. My initial reactions when God said NO; hurt, disappointment, and discouragement. However, as I reflect about my life, how are things turned out to be; I am very thankful and very grateful to God our Heavenly Father for protecting me from harm and danger. Every NO that I received from God was a blessing in disguise. I am thankful and grateful to God through Christ Jesus for placing me where I am today (a glorious place). God is good to me always. I truly believe that God loves those who trust Him for everything. It also shows that God is in control of everything and of our destiny. I can't help myself but to praise the Lord every day and every moment of my life. For every breath I take, I thank the Almighty God for guiding me to the path of righteousness, and I smile. O Lord my God, how awesome and wonderful you are.

It is my prayer that you too, may you find peace, joy, and comfort in God's love. Through Christ Jesus, may you find yourself and God's will for you. All you have to do is trust and believe in Jesus Christ and God's redemption for you through the cross. AMEN

Ephesians 1:7 In him we have redemption through his blood, the forgiveness of sins, in accordance with the riches of God's grace.

CHAPTER 5
ARE YOU ENJOYING LIFE TO THE FULLEST?

Ecclesiastes 3:11

He has made everything beautiful in his time: also he has set the world in their heart so that no man can find out the work that God makes from the beginning to the end.

Everything is as God made it, not as it appears to us. We have the world so much in our hearts, our thoughts and cares are filled with worldly things, that we have neither time nor spirit to see God's creation. The world has not only gained possession of the heart but has formed thoughts against the beauty of God's works. We are here to do good in this life, which is short and uncertain; we have but little time. Contentment with divine providence is having faith that all things work together for good to those who love him. Those who lack purpose and direction in life should respect God and follow His principles for living. Those who think life is unfair should remember that God will renew every person's life to determine how he/she responds to God. Does your life measure up to God's standard? Have you committed your life to our Lord and Saviour, Jesus Christ?

It's true we will sin and make mistakes, but we must never use this excuse to rebel against God's Word. (James 5:20 lets him know that whoever brings back a sinner from his wandering will save his soul from death and will cover a multitude of sins.) Do you allow yourself to go down a dark path and remain rebellious? Have courage, but do it kindly, humbly, and gently. Return to hope and praise, for the God who saved you also gave you a purpose and what you need to accomplish. It has never been about you or me, as much as you want to think it is. It is all about God's plan of eternal redemption, about the Lord's glory, about God's work, about God's kingdom, and our Lord God is big enough to handle the enemy and our feebleness.

Ecclesiastes 1:18

The greater my wisdom, the greater my grief. To increase knowledge only increases sorrow.

Sometimes, we feel that our eyes are fountain of tears. We are filled with emotions of disappointments and discouragements. We weep in despair, and our hearts bleed with sorrow. Gone are the melodies of birds singing. And our future seems bleak. God sees our troubles and hears our cries. We can rest in God's arms. In Jesus Christ alone, we have hope, and our future is bright. Rejoice every day, but remember that eternity is forever. A wise person does not think of the moment alone. It is a wonderful thing to be alive. Approach your decisions from an eternal perspective - consider the impact now and forever. Live a life with an attitude that although this life is short, we can live with God forever through our Lord and Saviour, Jesus Christ.

Ecclesiastes 4:4

Then I observed that most people are motivated to succeed because they envy their neighbours. But this, too, is meaningless–like chasing the wind.

Rather than looking to the world to patch up spiritual wounds, which it can never do, we should look to God to change our hearts. Nothing in this world will satisfy. Find satisfaction and joy in Christ, which remains forever. You can't try to substitute the joy found in Christ. All other joy is only temporary. The world has us comparing ourselves to each other. God says, "I'm going to be your confidence." It is important on our walk of faith that we get alone with God so we can allow God to work in us and through us in Christ Jesus. He never intended for you to look for confidence in yourself.

Give thanks in everything. Our joy, prayers, and thankfulness should not fluctuate with our situation. It doesn't mean we should give thanks FOR everything but IN everything. Evil does not come from God, so we should not thank Him for evil. But when evil strikes, we can still be thankful for who God is and for the good He can bring through distress. (1 Thessalonians 5:18 In everything give thanks: for this is the will of God in Christ Jesus concerning you.). When we do God's will, we will find it easier to be joyful and thankful.

Ecclesiastes 7:9

Be not hasty in thy spirit to be angry: for anger resteth in the bosom of fools.

Are we reacting to an evil situation or action that you are going to set right? Are we responding selfishly to a personal insult?

Scripture tells us that Christians should not name call others because it comes from unrighteous anger. Yes, that's why your name called. All the ways of Jesus are righteous, and He always has a just cause for calling someone a fool or a hypocrite. Refrain from unrighteous anger, be angry, and do not sin. The ultimate source of all encouragement is the fact that God is love, and He loves us and has a perfect plan for us. How comforting to know and have the assurance of God's unfailing love for us. When God takes priority in our lives; life becomes an adventure. Even our mundane routine takes on meaning and promise because they hold a greater purpose. If you're bored in life, check your relationship with GOD.

Afflictions - trouble, difficulties, and disappointments - occur in a sinful world. David said the righteous have many afflictions, though the Lord does deliver them. How you look at your troubles makes all the difference in the world! Do you think about them, talk about them, focus on them, and imagine a few extra? Do you let the devil drag your spirit down to the hell of depression and a defeated life?

Affliction is a devil that takes away your joy and fellowship with the Lord. Turn your needs over to the Lord with thanksgiving, and He will give you peace that passes human understanding. A person with a merry heart hardly knows he has afflictions. All he sees is God's glory, the blessings of life, and the hope of heaven! Hope is the life-spring of joy and believing that Jesus Christ came to give His children the abundant life.

Take no thought for tomorrow; He will take care of it for you. Don't be anxious, worried, or fearful. Look at the infinite God, who loves you as His dearly adopted child and Who is preparing a new home for you! Count your blessings! Name them one by one! There, you will find the fullness of joy and pleasures forevermore. King David said God's word was more valuable than gold, sweeter than honey, and brings great peace.

It is your choice to avoid the pain, darkness, and sorrow of a hopeless life. All the bad events that happen to the righteous are for only four reasons: the glory of God, the perfection of their faith, the chastening of their sins, or the consequences of their foolishness. Wisely considered, these are all good events! God's glory should be our constant goal; growth in faith is a great blessing; chastening is proof of God's love and for our profit; and consequences drive us to wisdom. Thank you, Lord, for bad events! (Psalm 19:7-14 The law of the Lord is perfect, converting the soul; The testimony of the Lord is sure, making wise the simple; 8 The statutes of the Lord are right, rejoicing the heart. The commandment of the Lord is pure, enlightening the eyes; 9 The fear of the Lord is clean, enduring forever; The judgments of the Lord are true and righteous altogether. 10 More to be desired are they than gold, Yea, than much fine gold, Sweeter also than honey and the honeycomb. 11 Moreover, by them,

Your servant is warned, and in keeping them there is a great reward.12. Who can understand his errors? Cleanse me from secret faults. 13 Keep back Your servant also from presumptuous sins; Let them not have dominion over me. Then I shall be blameless, And I shall be innocent of great transgression.14 Let the words of my mouth and the meditation of my heart Be acceptable in Your sight, O Lord, my strength and my Redeemer.)

A wise Christian only has good events in his life! If you know Jesus Christ as your Lord and Saviour, what else in the world could you want?

Ecclesiastes 5:10

"Whoever loves money never has enough; whoever loves wealth is never satisfied with their income."

To be content is to see life from God's point of view. Focus on our priorities and be grateful for everything God has given us. Often, our desire to have more and the longing to fill the empty place in our life to have more lead us to discontent. (Philippians 4:12 "I know what it is to be in need, and I know what it is to have plenty. I have learned the secret of being content in any and every situation, whether well fed or hungry, whether living in plenty or in want.") Do we have a great need, or are we discontent because we don't have what we want? How can we find true contentment? The answer lies in our perspective, priorities, and our source of power. The secret is Christ's power in us. Trusting that God will supply our every need.

Hear the stern warnings and dire predictions and commit yourself to honour God our Lord Jesus. This could free us from our scramble for power, approval, and money. We can never know enough to answer all of life's questions (Ecclesiastes 3:11), to predict our own future, or to manipulate God for our own ends. Life always has more questions than answers, and we must constantly go to God for fresh insights into life's dilemmas through Christ Jesus.

Being rich in this world is wholly different from being rich towards God. Nothing is more uncertain than worldly wealth. Those who are rich must see that God gives them their riches; and he only can give to enjoy them richly; for many have riches but enjoy them poorly, not having a heart to use them. (1 Timothy 6:20 O Timothy, keep that which is committed to your trust, avoiding profane and vain utterances and oppositions of what is falsely called knowledge.)

Ecclesiastes 12:13 Let us hear the conclusion of the whole matter: Fear God and keep His commandments, For this is man's all. 14 For God will bring every work into judgment, Including every secret thing, Whether good or evil.

CHAPTER 6
TRUST AND CONTENTMENT

Ecclesiastes 3:1-8

For everything, there is a season and a time for every matter under heaven: a time to be born, and a time to die; a time to plant, and a time to harvest; a time to kill, and a time to heal; a time to break down, and a time to build up; a time to cry, and a time to laugh; a time to mourn, and a time to dance; a time to keep, and a time to throw away; a time to find, a time to lose; a time to be quiet, a time to speak up; a time to tear, a time to repair; a time to love, a time to hate; a time for war, a time for peace; a time to embrace, and a time to refrain from embracing;

In my daily reading of God's word, I always learn something new. Trust and contentment. Humility helps us put others first and allow us to be content in God's leading in our lives. With such contentment, we do not need to prove ourselves to others but gives us security, freedom, and strength to serve God and others. trust for contentment teaches the importance of a humble and submissive temper; characteristics required for the making of 'true children of God.' The Lord Himself taught us to be meek and humble in spirit, and we should do all we can to be image-bearers of those Christ-like virtues. Do not deceive, thinking that we can hide from our sins. Sins rot us from the inside out, and our lives can be ruined. As one day, our sins will be exposed in plain sight. God knows each one's heart...live a life that is pleasing to God alone.

Throughout our lives, we are judged. For example, we are judged at school, when getting a driver's license, and at work, but it's never a problem. It's only a problem when it has to do with status (poverty). How are we to stay away from bad friends if we can't judge? If you remain rebellious towards His Word, you wouldn't want God to judge you. When using this excuse to justify willful sin goes wrong. How are we to watch out for false teachers if we can't judge? The truth is you wouldn't want God to judge you. God is a consuming fire. When He judges the wicked, He throws them into Hell for eternity. There will be no escaping the torment. Jesus didn't die, so you can spit on His grace and mock Him by your actions. Do you not care about the great price that Jesus paid for your soul.

Society has lost its grip on reality when people started believing in evolution as opposed to creations. When people neglected to acknowledge the creator (God) and put more emphasis on wealth and fame. People became mentally unstable when they started consulting with a 'medium' and reading horoscopes as opposed to reading the words of God (Bible). (Proverbs 3:5 Trust in the Lord with all thine heart; and lean not unto thine own understanding. 6 In all thy ways acknowledge him, and he shall direct thy paths.)

The bible has all the answers to everyday life's situations. Through Christ Jesus, we will have a firm foundation, stability, and the assurance of eternal life. Turn your eyes on our Lord Jesus Christ.

Ecclesiastes 5:12

The sleep of a labouring man is sweet, whether he eats little or much: but the abundance of the rich will not suffer him to sleep.

Do you ever think that if you become rich, all your problems would go away? From today's verse, we learn that wealth brings its own set of anxieties. Fear of theft and loss can rob a rich person of sleep and peace. But the one who is sustained with daily bread from the Lord rests in comfort, knowing that God meets all his needs. We are often troubled by the uncertainties of life. The fear of mountains crumbling into the sea by a nuclear blast sometimes plays in people's minds. God assures us that even to the world's ends, we need not fear. Let's express great confidence in God that he can save us. God is our refuge in the face of destruction. God gives us the strength to face uncertainties. God is not merely a temporary retreat; He is our eternal refuge. Our Lord Jesus Christ.

What is the best estate worth, more than as it gives opportunity of doing the better? Being rich in this world is wholly different from being rich towards God. Nothing is more uncertain than worldly wealth. Those who are rich must see that God gives them their riches; and he only can give to enjoy them richly; for many have riches, but enjoy them poorly, not having a heart to use them. (1 Timothy 6:20 O Timothy, keep that which is committed to your trust, avoiding profane and vain utterances and oppositions of what is falsely called knowledge.)

We all walk different paths of life...we all have struggles along the way. We trip, we fall, and get hurt. But, as long us we include God through our journey of life, all things are possible and become new. In the end, what we make of our life's experiences is what make us. We have everything we need...all we must do is believe.

Ecclesiastes 6:2

God gives some people wealth, possessions, and honor so that they lack nothing their hearts desire, but God does not grant them the ability to enjoy them, and strangers enjoy them instead. This is meaningless, a grievous evil.

We all want to be liked, so we are vulnerable to flattery, a dangerous trap. To avoid falling into it, be realistic about yourself. Know when you deserve praise and when you need to be rebuke. The knowledge and the wisdom can make you immune to flattery and protect you from being manipulated by the people who use it. Know who you are in God, and be confident of yourself. (Those who flatter their neighbors are spreading nets for their feet. Proverbs 29:5)

We need to stop worrying and stop being distracted by the world, and just listen to the Lord. Stop and drop everything; keep your focus on Christ Jesus. (Isaiah 40:31 But they that wait upon the LORD shall renew their strength; they shall mount up with wings as eagles; they shall run, and not be weary; and they shall walk, and not faint.) Life's challenges beset us once too many. The dark tunnel seems endless. We can't see where we are headed. Unexpected events can occur in a blink of an eye. Circumstances that could alter one's life, which will bring us to our knees and pray to God in despair. Perhaps, this is God's way of showing us to humble ourselves -- to be on our knees to pray and beg for grace and mercy.

As a human, we often forget what really matters in our lives. God should be our priority. As it is stated in the bible... (Matthew 6:33 But seek first the kingdom of God and His righteousness, and all these things shall be added to you.) Because God loves us; He finds a way for us to remain in His fold. (John 3:16 For God so loved the world that he gave his one and only Son, that whoever believes in him shall not perish but have eternal life.) Don't let pride deter you from obeying God and from following Jesus as your Lord and Saviour. Life is a mystery.... but God is the master of it. We pray for wisdom, prosperity, compassion, forgiveness and love. There are moments in our lives when we feel that no one cares. Through prayer, we can pull out of our present predicament. Be reminded that God cares for us deeply. (2 Samuel 22:33 It is God who arms me with strength and keeps my way secure.)

Happiness is not guaranteed in life. We must make it happen for ourselves. Our ability to find humor and laughter in any given situations is a gift to give ourselves. Let's face it: life is funny with its quirks and contradictions. To gain new perspectives to make others smile and laugh. Unlock our key to happiness with sense of humor. Let's look for humor in everything, in every circumstance, in every situation. Laugh more and live a happy life.

Ecclesiastes 12:13

"The end of the matter; all has been heard. Fear God and keep his commandments, for this is the whole duty of man."

No matter what we attain in life, death is eminent, the ultimate equalizer of all people. Hence, what we do here on earth has great impact upon where we spend our eternal life. We must not build our life on perishable pursuits but on solid foundation of God; even when everything we have is taken away, we still have God. (Revelation 14:13 And I heard a voice from heaven saying, "Write this: Blessed are the dead who die in the Lord from now on." "Blessed indeed," says the Spirit, "that they may rest from their labors, for their deeds follow them!")

Have you ever wondered what heaven looks like? What a wonderful truth: no matter what we are going through, God is the author of our life's final chapter. It is about the fulfillment and eternal joy for those who love Him. We do not know as much as we would like, but it is enough to know that eternity with God will be more wonderful than we can imagine. (Romans 5:2 through whom we have gained access by faith into this grace in which we stand. And we rejoice in the hope of the glory of God.)

Life is a journey, and it is filled with mystery. The depths of knowing what is to be not guaranteed. But God knows what our future holds. To find what you seek in the road of life, leave no stone unturned. Life has no smooth road for any of us, and in bracing atmosphere of a high aim, the very roughness stimulates the climber to steadier steps till the legend, over steep ways to the stars, fulfills itself. Let God be our guide in all that we do. When we trust and obey God....our future is upon thy Salvation....Everlasting Hope......Everlasting Future...Everlasting life. (Deuteronomy 31:6 Be strong and courageous. Do not fear or be in dread of them, for it is the Lord your God who goes with you. He will not leave you or forsake you.)

CHANGE....a word/action that alters life for better or for worse. Many of us want to make a change and move forward. Many don't want to or afraid to do so for the fear of the unknown tomorrow. The few who make changes can be overwhelming as the future is uncertain. The things we leave behind can deter us to step forward and face the unknown --- our future. Some purged and made a change, not knowing what the future holds. But trust in the Lord God Almighty, as He alone knows our future.

Ecclesiastes 10:10

If the ax is dull and its edge unsharpened, more strength is needed, but skill will bring success.

Expectations....We often have unrealistic expectations of others and of ourselves. And usually, when that happens, the outcome isn't so great. We feel disappointed, hurt, and resentful. Why it is that accepting things as they are and not having expectations is difficult to do. A battle we can never win is fighting within our own being as we set our hearts and minds to greater expectations. May we expect less from others and from ourselves but strive for a better good.

A blessed life is when you spend time with God along with your children and talk about how great God is. Knowing that your children are growing spiritually and are equipped with Spiritual Armor of God through Christ Jesus, who is their Lord and Savior. To God be all the glory. I praise the Lord Almighty forever. I am blessed beyond my expectations. Stop trusting in your own timing. Stop trying to accomplish God's plan in your own strength. Many times, God gives more than what is expected. God is able! We must never forget, though it is by His mercy and His grace. We deserve nothing, and everything is for His glory. May we find ways to be in constant obedient to God's leading in our lives. We are but mere human being, humbled by the grace and mercy.

Proverbs 11:24 One gives freely, yet grows all the richer; another withholds what he should give and only suffers want.

CHAPTER 7
ARE YOU GRATEFUL FOR EVERYTHING?

Ecclesiastes 11:8-9

8 Be grateful for every year you live. No matter how long you live, remember that you will be dead much longer. There is nothing at all to look forward to. 9 Young people, enjoy your youth. Be happy while you are still young. Do what you want to do and follow your heart's desire.

We often say life is complicated. Perhaps it is because we make it complicated by wanting to acquire more material things. Instead of enjoying the simple things in life and being grateful for what God hath blessed us with. We often say love is complicated. Perhaps it is because we love with condition. We expect much from those we love, and we are often disappointed. We complicate love as we often love with reservation.

We all travel a different path. In what we call a journey of life. Each path has its own obstacles, twists, and turns. A mountain to climb, a bridge to cross. It can be overwhelming. We feel discouraged and weary. When we fear to cross the bridge. When the mountain seems too steep to climb. God sees our troubled situations. Let us seek God first in all that we do. Our life's journey will be easy, and our burden will be light. God assures us He will carry us over troubled water. God will guide us to the green pasture. Where peace, hope, joy, and love await our arrival. And rest our weary soul in God's everlasting arms.

The world says hold on to as much as possible of our riches, but God blesses those who give freely. God supplies us with what we need to help others. In addition, giving helps us gain a right perspective on our possessions. We realize they were never really ours, to begin with, but were given to us by God to be used to help others. Freedom from enslavement to our possessions, the joy of helping others, and God's blessings.

In our society, we value assertiveness, and at times, it is a needed characteristic. However, assertiveness can become selfishness if not tempered by love. Doing things our way may call it assertiveness, but if God weights our actions, it may be considered selfish. Fine lines between assertiveness and selfishness....my way, your way, or God's way.

If you are happy and good and kind, you are already rich. After all, we came to this world without money, and we can not bring our money with us when we die. Most people still believe that money brings happiness. Most people craving greater riches can be caught in an endless cycle that only ends in ruin and destruction.

How can we keep away from the love of money?

The Bible teaches us some principles:

1) realize that one day, riches will be all gone.

2) be content with what we have

3) watch what are you willing to do to get more money

4) love people more than money

5) love doing God's work more than money

6) share freely what we have with others.

There is nothing wrong with having plenty or being rich, but it is wrong to worship our riches and money. Love God and love others.

Ecclesiastes 10:2

The heart of the wise inclines to the right, but the heart of the fool to the left.

Memories of God's goodness and faithfulness sustained us through our difficulties and during our trials and tribulations. We know God is able, and he is trustworthy. When we face new trials, let us review the good things that God has done in our lives, and this will strengthen our faith. (Psalms 77:11-12. "I will remember the deeds of the Lord; yes, I will remember your miracles of long ago. I will consider all your works and meditate on all your mighty deeds.") God is simply saying to give wholeheartedly, not grudgingly. When we give, God supplies us with more so we can give more. In addition, giving help us gain a right perspective on our possessions. We realize they were never really ours to begin with, but given to us by God to be used to help others. Each day I rise is a blessing in itself. Some days are better than other days; nevertheless, I am blessed. For each day held a memory to cherish for a lifetime through. Each day, I pray that my life and that my characters will be worthy to emulate. Holy and acceptable to God. Each day, I am thankful for everything. Each day, I just trust God our Heavenly Father that He will walk with me, to give me eyes to see goodness and beauty in all that I see.

Life's challenges beset us once too many. The dark tunnel seems endless. We can't see where we are headed. Unexpected events can occur in a blink of an eye. Circumstances that could alter one's life, which will bring us to our knees and pray to God in despair. Perhaps, this is God's way of showing us to humble ourselves -- to be on our knees to pray and beg for grace and mercy. As a human, we often forget what really matters in our lives. God should be our priority. As it is stated in the bible... (Matthew 6:33 But seek first the kingdom of God and His righteousness, and all these things shall be added to you.) Because God loves us; He finds a way for us to remain in His fold. (John 3:16 For God so loved the world that he gave his one and only Son, that whoever believes in him shall not perish but have eternal life.)

Ecclesiastes 4:1-3

1 Again, I saw all the oppressions that are done under the sun. And behold, the tears of the oppressed, and they had no one to comfort them! On the side of their oppressors, there was power, and there was no one to comfort them. 2 And I thought the dead who are already dead more fortunate than the living who are still alive. 3 But better than both is he who has not yet been and has not seen the evil deeds that are done under the sun.

There are those days when we rise from our slumber; Our heart is already heavily laden with burdens and cares. Our mind is already preoccupied with an overwhelming day of struggles and hardships. Nevertheless, we can be assured that everything we needed God has provided. We can be thankful and count our blessings. I pray that when we are overwhelmed with trials, hardships, and daily struggles may we remember that God doesn't send us extraordinary trials.... without extraordinary blessings. (James 1:2 Count it all joy, my brothers when you meet trials of various kinds, for you know that the testing of your faith produces steadfastness. And let steadfastness have its full effect, that you may be perfect and complete, lacking in nothing.)

We will face unpleasantness and life's daily challenges. Our heart is already heavily laden with burdens and cares. Our mind is already preoccupied with overwhelming days of struggles and hardships. Nevertheless, we can be assured that everything we needed God has provided. We do not know what tomorrow brings, but we can be thankful and count our blessings. Abraham never doubted that God would fulfill his promise. His life was marked by mistakes, sins, and failures, as well as wisdom and goodness. But he consistently trusted God. His life was an example of faith in action. (Romans 4:20 Yet he did not waver through unbelief regarding the promise of God but was strengthened in his faith and gave glory to God). Let us appreciate God's timing.... because timing is everything in God's plans.

We live in a broken and sinful world full of broken and sinful people. It is comforting to know that God isn't ever broken. God isn't ever caught off guard or surprised by what happening in the world. He is going to work in us humility, kindness, mercy, long-suffering, and more. How can you grow in patience if you are never in a situation where patience is needed? Trials change us, and they fix our eyes on eternity. They make us more thankful.

Ecclesiastes 4:7-8

7 Again, I saw vanity under the sun: 8 one person who has no other, either son or brother, yet there is no end to all his toil, and his eyes are never satisfied with riches, so that he never asks, "For whom am I toiling and depriving myself of pleasure?" This also is vanity and an unhappy business.

May the splendour of the Lord and the Glory of God shine upon us today. May our day be filled with love, hope, and peace. Our God is an awesome God. May he wrap his loving arms around us as we go through life's daily struggles. There is a blessed assurance that God is with us always. In every trial, God is there with us...always...I am in the hands of the Holy Spirit. I experience the awesome reality of living in the faith. I know that the Holy Spirit is directing me in all that I do. I perceive everything as pleasant... even if it's sometimes unpleasant. I see my identity as a Divine being unfolding in the hands of GOD. I live with the understanding that by remaining open and empty. GOD can manifest and shine through me. I am grateful to be Alive...I know I am loved by GOD.......My Lord and Saviour Jesus Christ. (Psalm 96:6 "Splendor and majesty are before Him, Strength and beauty are in His sanctuary.") God is our constant protection, and he is limitless. When we find ourselves in need of God's protection, let's take it to the Lord in prayer. God is our strength, our fortress, and our deliverer. He is our salvation, and we can trust him. Praise God for his glorious works and constant blessings.

Ecclesiastes 4:6

There was no end of all the people, all of whom he led. Yet those who come later will not rejoice in him. Surely this also is vanity and a striving after wind.

Just when we thought everything is fine and dandy, somehow, God always finds a way to remind us of and to show us that He always commands our destiny. Lest we get the wrong idea, we are not the sovereign masters of our fate. Only God is sovereign. His sovereign control is called "Providence." He has chosen to give us a free will, and He has created a moral universe in which the law of cause-and-effect is a reality. But God is God alone, and there are no "accidents" in the universe. An all-wise, all-powerful God must have a plan, so it should be no surprise that the Bible speaks of a divine plan. God's plan, since it belongs to God, is holy, wise, and benevolent. The providence of God is working to bring about His original plan for creation. The Lord has a plan for each child, born or unborn.

(Job 3:20 Wherefore is light given to him that is in misery, and life unto the bitter in soul). Misery somehow besets us once too many in our lifetime. However, as we pour out our miseries; God only hears melodies. As we honestly cry with breaking heart; God hears our plea and feels our pain. During our sadness/sorrow; may we find God's joy. In our storms of life, may we find God's peace. In our darkest moment and when hope seems so bleak; may we find God's light, life, and most of all LOVE through Christ Jesus. Let us then look at our life through heaven's eyes, and may we remember Christ suffered greatly for us. As we look at the cross and the empty grave; remember then that God's will should be our will. God and

God alone shape our future and controls our destiny. Let God be God.

God is mysteriously unfathomable. Often, what we do not understand we theorize. And if our theory does not fit our perception., we either accept the fact that God is God, and we are not, or we completely deny and ignore the truth, and we continue to seek what is true. In our despair and frustration, we either embrace that JESUS CHRIST IS GOD OR deny the fact that He died on the cross for our salvation. Did we ever stop for a moment and contemplate how our Saviour could survive such torture? The lashing he received could have killed him due to blood loss; dehydration could have killed him. Being crucified caused asphyxiation. He was buried, and in three days, he rose again. (Colossians 1:10 Then the way you live will always honour and please the Lord and your lives will produce every kind of good fruit. All the while, you will grow as you learn to know God better and better.) The spirit, body, and soul are an integral part of a person. God must be involved in every aspect of our lives. 3 John 1:2 Beloved, I pray that you may prosper in all things and be in health, just as your soul prospers.

Ephesians 1:4 Even before he made the world, God loved us and chose us in Christ to be holy and without fault in his eyes.

CHAPTER 8
TAKE NOTHING FOR GRANTED

Ecclesiastes 9:5

"For the living know that they will die, but the dead know nothing."

We are often troubled by the uncertainties of life. The fear of mountains crumbling into the sea by a nuclear blast sometimes plays in people's minds. God assures us that even to the world's ends, we need not fear. Let's express great confidence in God that he can save us. God is our refuge in the face of destruction. God gives us the strength to face uncertainties. God is not merely a temporary retreat; He is our eternal refuge. Our Lord Jesus Christ. God's awesome and wonderful power is not restricted to creating scenic wonders; he also uses it to execute righteousness and justice. It is not enough to be awed by God's power. We need discipline to learn how to obey and live for Jesus Christ.

God did not promise that all His followers will be wealthy (materially). When God pardons, He restores our relationship with Him, not individual wealth. Instead, God promises to meet the deepest needs of those who love Him - if not immediately now, certainly in eternity. Trusting in God's hand one day at a time, step-by-step, you will grow in deeper maturity in Christ. With the help of the Holy Spirit, keep in step with the godly man/woman in you. You can put your trust in God not only for eternal life but also for purpose and direction for life on this earth. Beneath the surface of the routine of daily life, a fierce struggle among invisible spiritual powers is being waged. Like the wind, the evil powers force can be devastating. Our main defence is a prayer that God will protect us from evil and that He will make us strong. We are constantly confronted with temptations to turn away from God. We should hold on to the truth found in Jesus Christ's teaching because our lives depend on it. Never forget the reality of Christ's life and love for us.

Some people think worldliness has to do with external behaviour ---the people we associate with, the places we go, and the activities in which we participate. This is entirely not accurate, for worldliness begins in the heart. (1 John 2:15-17 Stop loving the world and the things that are in the world. If anyone persists in loving the world, the Father's love is not in him. For everything that is in the world—the desire for fleshly gratification, the desire for possessions, and worldly arrogance—is not from the Father but is from the world. And the world and its desires are fading away, but the person who does God's will remains forever.)

It is characterized by these three attitudes:

1) LUST --- preoccupation with gratifying physical desire.

2) MATERIALISM --- craving and accumulating things

3) PRIDE --- obsession with one's status or importance. When the serpent tempted Eve (Genesis 3:6), he tempted her in these areas. When the devil tempted Jesus in the wilderness, these were his three areas of attack (Matthew 4:1-11).

God values self-control, a spirit of generosity, and a humble service. It is possible to avoid "worldly pleasures" while still harbouring a worldly attitude in one's heart. When our attachment to things is strong, it is hard to believe that the things we want will one day pass away. It may even be hard to believe that the person who does the will of God will live forever. Knowing that this evil world and its sin will end will give us the courage to continue doing God's will. Live and love as our Lord and Saviour Jesus Christ; he loves and spends time with sinners while maintaining the values of God's Kingdom. What values are most important to you? Do your actions reflect the world's values or God's values? Will you fail like Eve did or be victorious like our Lord Jesus Christ?

What kind of crops are we sowing today? What is the long-term effect of our actions? Each day, we must deal with our share of earthly burdens. As we face these burdens, the Lord is there to help us bear them. Each morning, praise God for the strength He will send us today; it is as sure as the sunrise. We should feel overwhelming awe as we kneel before the Lord. Surrounding us with countless signs of His majesty. Unlimited power and unspeakable majesty leave us breathless in His presence. When we catch our breath, praise God. When we think of reaping what we sow, we often think of negative results. However, we can expect both positive and negative results. Plow the hard ground of our heart by opening it to God for forgiveness. Just as the small seeds eventually produce large crops. Our everyday small actions can produce far-reaching results for good or for evil. Let our lives be ready and available for God to work in it by sowing the spirit of love; hence, we can reap love and joy.

Ecclesiastes 7:1-4

1 A good name is better than fine perfume, and the day of death better than the day of birth. 2 It is better to go to a house of mourning than to go to a house of feasting, for death is the destiny of everyone; the living should take this to heart. 3 Frustration is better than laughter because a sad face is good for the heart. 4 The heart of the wise is in the house of mourning, but the heart of fools is in the house of pleasure.

GOD declared we are valuable to HIM. We can be set free from feeling unworthiness. The greatness of God assures the worth of mankind. God, the all-powerful creator, cares for His most valuable creation---YOU....as Jesus Christ died for YOU!!!!

To enjoy what God has given us, we are to enjoy what we have while we can but realize that adversity also strikes. Adversity reminds us that life is short, teaches us to live wisely, and refines our character. Most would agree that we learn more about God from difficult times than from happy times. See sorrows and struggles as a great opportunity to learn from God.

Many people avoid thinking about death and refuse to face it. King Solomon was not encouraging to think morbidly, but it is helpful at times to think about death. It reminds us that there is still time to change. Time to examine the direction of our lives and time to confess our sins and find forgiveness. Everyone will eventually die. It makes sense to plan and experience God's mercy rather than his justice. (Deuteronomy 28:1 If you fully obey the Lord your God and carefully follow all his commands I give you today, the Lord your God will set you high above all the nations on earth.) Walk with the Lord in obedience even if we do not know what lays ahead. Faith is something that we do even when we do not know the outcome, but the Lord God Almighty does. It gives me such joy to see that the Lord our God is at work in people's lives that He brought to us. When we give everything to God in prayer and trust that everything will be alright. Our burden will be light, and our spirit will be lifted up through Jesus Christ, who daily bears our burdens. Always be humble and always trust God, for He knows what is best for us. I am where I am because this is where the Lord needs me to be in this such as time. (Acts 5:32 We are witnesses of these things, and so is the Holy Spirit, whom God has given to those who obey him.) God changed our position to change our perspective. Each change brings another opportunity for God to change our perspective.

Ecclesiastes 7:5-6

5 It is better to heed the rebuke of a wise person than to listen to the song of fools. 6 Like the crackling of thorns under the pot, so is the laughter of fools. This too is meaningless.

Don't waste God's gifts. Without dependence on God and his guidance, even great ability is wasted. Even now of great success, our pride and personal weaknesses are our greatest challenges. God has a purpose for every life, which becomes a real adventure for those who are willing to obey him wholeheartedly. When our attention is focused on God rather than our problems, God can help in unexpected ways. God's plan weaves live together in a pattern beyond our understanding. God uses our mistakes to fit into his plans.

Have you ever paid a compliment knowing it was inappropriate and merely an attempt to flatter you. Some people would rather feel good than know the truth. Pleasant compliments are too often valued above helpful information. (Proverbs 27:6 Wounds from a friend can be trusted, but an enemy multiplies kisses.) King Solomon reminds us that it is far better to face honest criticism than to wallow in the compliments of fools.

God is always in control of all that we desire. May it be for good of all that, in the end, we may find ourselves glorifying God. For we are created to glorify God. Let us then love one another as God is love. Let love be our guide in all that we do and speak. As we aspire to lead people, we need to be in unity. We are being tested with our faith with one another, and we are letting the darkness win.

When God starts a project, he finishes it. God will work in you and help you grow in grace until he has completed his work in your life. When you are discouraged, remember that God won't give up on you; He promises to finish the work he has begun. Let God do it. God's works for us began when Jesus died on the cross to forgive our sins. His works in us begin when the Holy Spirit comes into our hearts, enabling us to be more like Christ every day.

Ecclesiastes 7:7-8

7 Extortion turns a wise person into a fool, and a bribe corrupts the heart. 8 The end of a matter is better than its beginning, and patience is better than pride.

Money talks, and it can confuse those who would otherwise judge fairly. We hear about bribes given to judge. Bribes are given to hurt those who tell the truth and help those who oppose. The person who takes the bribe is indeed a fool, no matter how wise he thought he was before. Some say that everyone has his price, but those who are truly wise cannot be bought at any price. Dig and find God's treasure. Become spiritually rich through Jesus Christ. (2 Corinthians 8:9 For ye know the grace of our Lord Jesus Christ, that, though he was rich, yet for your sakes he became poor, that ye through his poverty might be rich.). They are yours to enjoy---Colossians 1:27 To whom God would make known what are the riches of the glory of this mystery among the Gentiles; which is Christ in you, the hope of glory: ---Colossians 2:2-3 That their hearts might be comforted, being knit together in love, and unto all riches of the full assurance of understanding, to the acknowledgment of the mystery of God, and of the Father, and of Christ; 3 In whom are hidden all the treasures of wisdom and knowledge. When God starts a project, he finishes it. God will work in you and help you grow in grace until he has completed his work in your life. When you are discouraged, remember that God won't give up on you; He promises to finish the work he has begun. Let God do it. God's works for us began when Jesus died on the cross to forgive our sins. His works in us begin when the Holy Spirit comes into our hearts, enabling us to be more like Christ every day.

Ecclesiastes 7:11-12

Wisdom, like an inheritance, is a good thing and benefits those who see the sun. 12 Wisdom is a shelter as money is a shelter, but the advantage of knowledge is this: Wisdom preserves those who have it.

To finish what we start takes hard work, wise guidance, and self discipline. Anyone with vision can start a big project, but vision without wisdom often results in unfinish projects or goals. It results to poverty and not prosperity. God created us to be dominion over everything, to be fruitful, and multiply. However, we often misinterpret God's messages to us knowingly or unknowingly. (Proverbs 11:24-25 There is one who scatters yet increases more; And there is one who withholds more than is right, But it leads to poverty. 25 The generous soul will be made rich, and he who waters will also be watered himself.)

Paul had faced excruciating poverty, abundant wealth, and everything in between. Paul wrote this letter from prison. Whatever the circumstance, Paul had learned to be content (4: 11.12), finding real joy as he focused all his attention and energy on knowing Christ (3:8) and obeying Him (3:12, 13). Paul's desire to know Christ above all else is wonderfully expressed in the following words: "Everything else is worthless when compared with the priceless gain of knowing Jesus Christ my Lord. I have put aside all else, counting it worth less than nothing. What do we want more of? Do we want more of God or his blessings? We often do what we thought is good and pleasing to God to receive more of his blessings. However, we miss the true meaning of blessings. Consider for a moment our faith and belief of who God is. The more we yearn for God, the more the blessings will overflow. Want more of God than his blessings. True faith is trusting God for the things yet seen. (Proverbs 10: 7 The memory of the righteous is a blessing, but the name of the wicked shall rot.)

We don't control or hold what tomorrow brings; thus, we live our life for Christ Jesus as if today is our last day on earth. But plan as if we live for more days to come. Trust in the Lord Jesus Christ for everything. There are so many things in this world that are beyond our control. God said to have faith, trust Him, and take everything to Him in prayer.

Psalm 46:1-3

1 God is our refuge and strength, A very present help in trouble. 2 Therefore we will not fear, even though the earth be removed, And though the mountains be carried into the midst of the sea; 3 Though its waters roar and be troubled, Though the mountains shake with its swelling.

CONCLUSION:

Ecclesiastes 12:13-14

13 That's the whole story. Here now is my final conclusion: Fear God and obey his commands, for this is everyone's duty. 14 God will judge us for everything we do, including every secret thing, whether good or bad.

The book of Ecclesiastes cannot be interpreted correctly without reading these final verses. We are not exempt from obeying God's commands. We should search for the purpose and meaning of life, but they can not be found in human endeavours. We should acknowledge the evil, foolishness, and injustice in life yet maintain a positive and strong faith in God. No matter what the mysteries and apparent contradictions of life, we must work toward the single purpose of knowing God our Lord Jesus Christ.

Everyone will stand before the Lord God Almighty and be judged for what they did in this life. We will not be able to use life's excuses for failing to live life properly. To properly live life, we need to: 1) recognize that human effort apart from God is futile, 2) put God first - NOW, 3) receive everything good from God, 4) realize that God judges both good and evil, 5) know that God will judge the quality of every person's life. How strange that people spent their lives striving for the very enjoyment that God gives freely as a gift...Eternal Life through Jesus Christ.

I love new beginnings; plenty of things to look forward to. And plenty of unknown challenges. One thing is for sure: God is the same yesterday, today, and tomorrow. God's living presence is our greatest joy. His radiant appearance helps us grow in strength, grace, and glory. May we constantly seek refuge in God. It is my prayer that love will always dwell in our hearts. As we search for God's guidance each day. May we find peace, hope, joy, and prosperity. Be grateful and be thankful in everything, and take nothing for granted. We have so much to be thankful for ---family, friends, but most of all, God sent us Christ Jesus, God's love, and mercy. We must trust the Holy Spirit to help us to overcome hardship and poverty. We can overcome poverty through determination, diligence, and hard work. Being faithful and constant in prayers. When we fully give ourselves to God, we will be blessed abundantly more than we can ask or imagine.

Long before my parents knew each other, the Lord our God knows me already. I thank God each day for everything......family and friends. 50+ years ago, my heavenly Father placed me in the palms of my earthly parents to care and nurture. I am thankful for everything that my parents did or didn't do, for it shaped me to who I am and what I'd become. I am where I am because of my parents. I thank God for them for nurturing me. (Jeremiah 1:5 "I knew you before I formed you in your mother's womb. Before you were born, I set you apart and appointed you as my prophet to the nations.") God already planned my future and authored my life's biography. My walk here on earth has never been easy, I faced many disappointments, hurts, defeats, hardships, and sorrows. God did not promise life to be easy. But Jesus said, come to me, I will give you rest.... victory in Jesus' name. Through Jesus Christ, who gives me strength, each day I rise from my slumber; I find hope, joy, and peace beyond human understanding. I am not perfect; I am forgiven. I believe God isn't finished yet, shaping me into the woman that He wants me to be. Hence, each day I put my faith and trust in God's hands through Christ Jesus...beautiful life.... (Jeremiah 29:11 For I know the plans I have for you," says the Lord. "They are plans for good and not for disaster, to give you a future and a hope.)

A Simple Sinner's Prayer ("For all have sinned and fall short of the glory of God" Romans 3:23)

Dear Heavenly Father, I come to you in the name of Jesus Christ. I acknowledge to You that I am a sinner, and I am sorry for my sins and the life that I have lived; I need your forgiveness.

I believe that your only Son, Jesus Christ, shed His precious blood on the cross at Calvary and died for my sins, and I am now willing to repent, confess, and turn from my sin. You said in the bible that if I confess the Lord our God and believe in my heart that God raised Jesus from the dead, I shall be saved.

I confess Jesus Christ as my Lord and my Saviour. With my heart, I believe that God raised Jesus from the dead. This very moment, I accept Jesus Christ as my own personal Savior, and according to His Word, right now I am saved. Amen.

www.ingramcontent.com/pod-product-compliance
Lightning Source LLC
Chambersburg PA
CBHW070337120526
44590CB00017B/2927